SCHOLASTIC SCIENCE READERS™

LEVEL
3
AGES 7 AND 8

# Rocks and Minerals

Edward R. Ricciuti

SCHOLASTIC
REFERENCE

The cover image is quartz.
The title page shows pyrite, sometimes called fool's gold.

ISBN 0-439-26993-8

*Book design by Barbara Balch and Kay Petronio*
*Photo research by Sarah Longacre*

10 9 8 7                              03 04

Printed in the U.S.A.     23

First printing, October 2001

We are grateful to Francie Alexander, reading specialist, and to Adele M. Brodkin, Ph.D., developmental psychologist, for their contributions to the development of this series.

Our thanks also to our science consultant Jeffrey Post, a research scientist and curator of the National Gem and Mineral Collection at the Smithsonian Institution.

Wherever you live, the biggest **rock** on Earth is right under your feet. It is Earth itself. If you are sitting on grass or walking on the sidewalk, you might not realize that you live on a rock. Our entire planet Earth is actually a huge ball of rock. Inside, it is made up of layers. The outer layer is the crust. We live on the crust's surface.

Earth's crust is solid rock. It is about 5 to 25 miles (8 to 40 kilometers) deep. If you think that sounds thick, think again. The crust is only Earth's skin. It is like the peel on the outside of an apple. The layers below the crust are much thicker.

*The Grand Canyon was formed when the Colorado River carved deep into Earth's crust.*

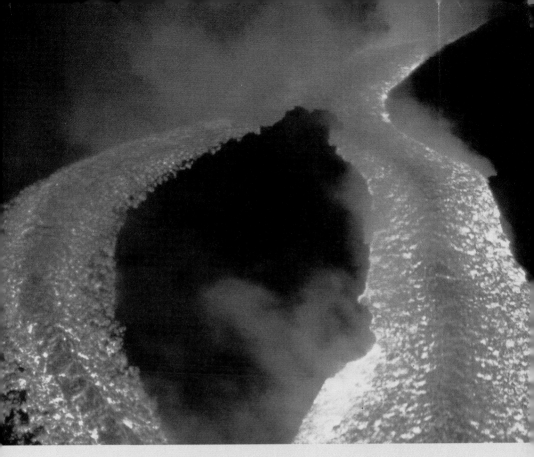

*Hot rock from the mantle can reach Earth's surface during a volcanic eruption.*

Under the crust lies the mantle, which is 1,800 miles (2,896 kilometers) thick. Rock there is sizzling hot. Deep in the mantle, the temperature can be as high as 5,000°F (2,760°C). Most rock in the mantle is soft but solid, like candle wax. Sometimes, rock in the mantle melts and becomes magma.

Beneath the mantle is the outer core. This layer is even hotter than the mantle. Temperatures there are higher than 7,000°F (3,871°C). It is so hot in the outer core that the rock is liquid, like honey. The outer core is 1,300 miles (2,092 kilometers) thick.

Finally, at the center of Earth is the inner core. It is solid, like the seed in a cherry.

If you compared the size of Earth to a basketball, the inner core would only be about the size of a tennis ball. When you are standing in your house, the inner core is about 3,100 miles (5,166 kilometers) beneath your feet.

*Earth's inner core*

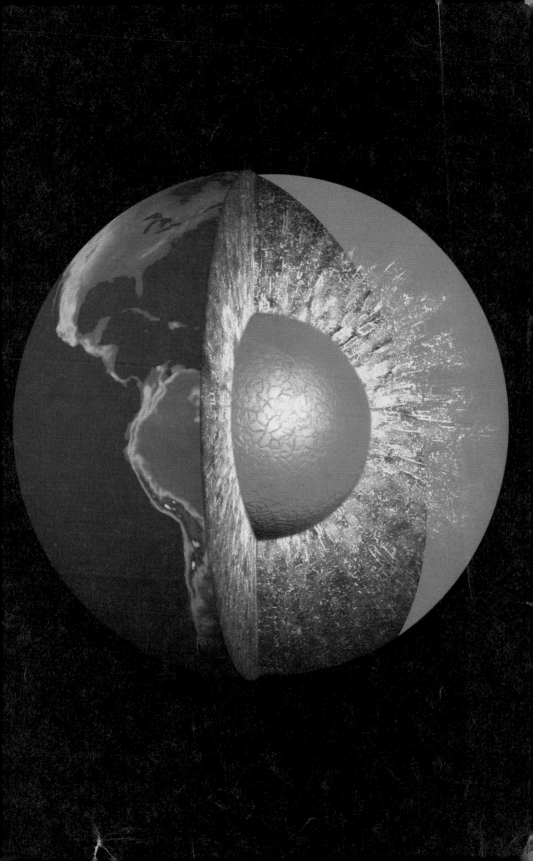

Not all of the rock on Earth is the same. There are hundreds of different kinds of rocks. What makes one rock different from another? Each kind of rock has its own special recipe. The ingredients of rock recipes are **minerals**.

A few rocks are made of only one mineral. Most are a mix of different minerals.

Rocks form when minerals join together. This usually happens when hot, liquid rock cools and hardens. However, some rocks form when **pressure** (**presh**-ur) from overlying rocks squeezes minerals and particles such as sand grains together.

*Towering granite walls in California's Kings Canyon National Park formed from a mixture of minerals.*

Minerals are made of simple chemicals (**kem**-uh-kuhlz) called elements. Some minerals contain only one element. Carbon is the only element in the mineral diamond. But most minerals are a combination of elements. Quartz is a common mineral made of the elements oxygen and silicon.

Minerals form as crystals. The shape of a crystal is a clue to a mineral's identity. Most diamond crystals have eight flat sides. The crystals of the mineral olivine look like marbles.

**clear quartz**

**milky quartz**

**rose quartz**

*A scientist measures a giant quartz crystal.*

Crystals are not alive. But they can grow in size. As more minerals attach to a crystal, it gets bigger. A crystal can be as large as a golf ball or even a baseball. Some are much larger.

Crystals can weigh hundreds of tons (metric tons). These crystals may have taken hundreds or millions of years to form. However, most crystals are smaller. Some are only the size of a pencil eraser. Others are even tinier and can only be seen with a microscope.

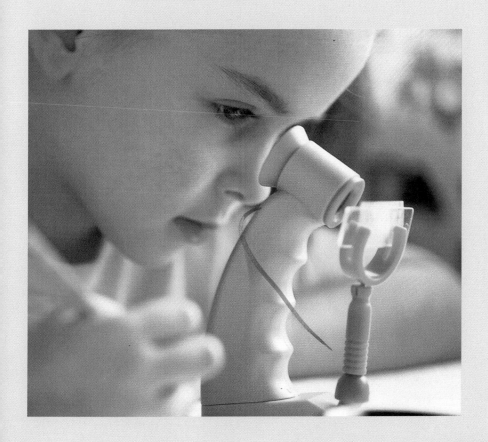

Mineral crystals are often very beautiful. Crystals of mica glint in the sun. Gypsum looks like ice and sparkles in light. Many crystals are gorgeous colors. Jadeite is green as grass and rhodonite is a pretty pink.

Some kinds of minerals are made into jewelry and precious gems. Gold and silver are minerals. They are soft and can be worked into different shapes to make necklaces, rings, and other jewelry.

**gold nugget**

*Rubies in their raw form* (left) *and a polished ruby gemstone* (right)

Rubies are gemstones from a mineral called corundum. Normally, this mineral is clear, without color. When the element chromium is trapped within corundum as it grows, it turns deep red and becomes a ruby, a precious gemstone.

*This rough diamond formed deep inside Earth.*

One of the most valuable gemstones is a diamond. A diamond forms when the element carbon is exposed to the extremely high heat and pressure of Earth's upper mantle. There are only a few places on Earth where there is enough heat and pressure to make diamonds. South Africa is one of these places.

A diamond found in nature can be very beautiful. But it becomes a thing of wonder when an expert turns it into a gem. Diamond cutters are experts who know how to cut, grind, and polish natural diamonds into jewels. Once cut and polished, diamonds catch and reflect light better than most other gems.

People use minerals every day, although they may not know it. Even precious minerals such as diamonds have practical uses. Diamond is the hardest mineral on Earth. Tools made of diamond can cut materials such as steel.

Gold is so long-lasting that it was once used as a filling for cavities in teeth. The salt you use on your food is actually the mineral halite. Grains of salt are halite crystals.

*The diamond tip of this tool is used to cut glass.*

Inside Earth, rocks continually form from minerals. Most rocks are recycled from others. Earth does not waste rocks. It makes new rocks from old ones.

*Swirls of sandstone, a sedimentary rock, can be found in Utah.*

Rocks are grouped into three classes: **igneous** (**ig**-nee-uhss) rock, **metamorphic** (*met*-uh-**mor**-fik) rock, and **sedimentary** (*sed*-uh-**men**-tuh-ree) rock. Igneous rocks are the hardest rocks. Metamorphic rocks are not quite as hard. Sedimentary rocks are the softest rocks. The name of each class of rock tells how it was formed.

"Igneous" means fire. Igneous rock starts out as melted rock deep within Earth. This hot goo is called magma. It often pushes up into the crust from below. When it breaks through the surface, it is known as lava. A breakthrough is called an eruption.

Eventually, magma and lava cool and harden. The result is igneous rock. Magma cools slowly. Hardening may take thousands or millions of years. Lava cools quickly and sometimes hardens in just a few minutes to a few days.

Lava often erupts in the same place over and over again. When this happens, the lava piles up into a volcano.

Different types of igneous rocks are formed depending on whether they start as lava or magma. Igneous rock that is formed from lava is called volcanic rock.

Igneous rock that is formed from magma is called plutonic rock. Pluto was the ancient Roman god of the underworld, so it made sense to name an underground type of rock after him.

*Lava formed Washington's Mount Rainier long ago, and continues to do so today.*

Volcanic rocks usually have tiny crystals. A few have no crystals at all. Obsidian, which is one of these, is smooth and glassy. Obsidian lacks crystals because it cools so fast that crystals have no time to grow.

Basalt (buh-**sawlt**) is a common rock formed from lava. Much of the floor of the ocean is made of basalt.

*Pillow lava forms when hot lava pushes up through the ocean floor.*

*Close-up of pumice*

One of the most unusual volcanic rocks is pumice (**puhm**-iss), which forms from foamy lava. Air pockets in pumice make it very light—so light that it can float on water.

*Granite may be different colors, depending on the minerals in it.*

Rocks formed underground from magma usually have larger crystals because magma cools very slowly and the crystals have more time to grow.

Granite is a common plutonic rock that often contains shiny crystals of quartz, mica, and feldspar.

Like most kinds of igneous rock, granite is very hard. Earth's continents are made primarily of granite. Granite is used as a building material because of its hardness.

*The U.S. Gold Depository at Fort Knox is made of granite.*

Even the hardest rock does not last forever. Water and wind wear it away. Parts of it break off. Some are big chunks, while others are as tiny as sand grains. Particles of rock are whirled by wind, swirled by water, flushed by rain into streams and lakes, and washed into the sea.

Sand grains were once part of rocks. They will become rock again. If you see sand being swept down a stream or into a storm drain, you are seeing the remains of old rocks. These particles are called sediment. The word means "to settle." That's exactly what sediment does. It settles to the sea bottom. There, it becomes sedimentary rock, the second major type of rock.

Unique rock formations in Utah's Grand Staircase–Escalante
National Monument show the effects of wind and water on rock.

Sediment also piles up on lake bottoms and on land. It can become sedimentary rock in these places, too. Rock particles are not the only ingredient in sedimentary rock. Sometimes it contains seashells, pebbles, and sand.

Sediment settles in layers, and these layers pile up. Layers on top press down on those below, making buried bits and pieces of sediment stick together. Eventually, they are squeezed into rock.

Sedimentary rock is a common surface rock on Earth. It is often seen where a highway has been cut through hills or mountains. Layers of sedimentary rock are clearly visible in road cuts.

*Close-up of conglomerate rock*

Sandstone, a sedimentary rock, is just what its name says—stone made of sand. Quartz is the main mineral in sandstone, but a few other minerals may be present, too.

Conglomerate (kon-**glom**-uh-rate), another sedimentary rock, is a mixture of pebbles naturally cemented together. The minerals in conglomerate depend on the pebbles it contains.

Limestone is made mainly of the mineral calcite. Calcite in limestone comes from the shells of ancient sea creatures. You probably have seen limestone in your classroom. Chalk, a very soft sedimentary rock, is a form of limestone.

*England's famous White Cliffs of Dover are made of limestone.*

Often, limestone has shells in it. These shells are **fossils**. A fossil is the remains of a prehistoric plant or animal, preserved in rock. Sedimentary rocks contain many of these remains.

## Take a Closer Look

*A fossil of an* Apatosaurus *leg bone*

*Amazing dinosaur fossils were found at
Dinosaur National Monument in Utah.*

Fossils form in many ways. Dinosaurs lived on Earth more than 65 million years ago. When a dinosaur died, it did not always disappear forever. Its body may have been buried in a landslide during a flood. Sediment piled up over it and became rock. Minerals from the rock entered the dinosaur's bones. They turned to stone and became fossils.

*Ancient plants left fossil imprints that still exist today.*

Evidence of plant life from long ago can also be found in sedimentary rocks. About 150 million years ago, ancient plants grew. They decayed, but their imprints were left in the sediment. When the sediment became rock, the imprints became fossils.

Many ancient life forms turned into fossils. They range in size from micro-organisms (mye-kroh-**or**-guh-niz-uhms) that can only be seen under a microscope to huge dinosaurs and whales.

Almost all fossils are found in sedimentary rocks. Layers of sedimentary rock can be like pages in the story of ancient life. Scientists read the layers like a history book.

Fossils of sea creatures found in sedimentary rock on land, for example, are a clue that an ocean once covered that area. By examining different fossils found in rock from the same time period, scientists can create a picture of the plants and animals living at that time.

The third type of rock is called metamorphic rock. "Metamorphic" comes from a word that means change. Metamorphic rock can be made from sedimentary rock or from igneous rock. Metamorphic rock can also be made from other metamorphic rocks.

*Gneiss is one kind of metamorphic rock.*

*Two very different forms of the same element—carbon*

Exposure to very high temperatures and very strong pressure can change one kind of rock into another. Heat and pressure change rocks just as those forces change minerals.

*Two different types of marble were used in the Lincoln Memorial.*

When limestone, a sedimentary rock, is squeezed, its calcite crystals pack together. The limestone changes to marble, a metamorphic rock. Marble is harder than limestone. But it is still soft enough to be carved into statues. Some of the world's most famous statues are made of marble.

Slate is a metamorphic rock. At one time, blackboards were made of slate. Slate is hard enough to write on with chalk. But slate starts out as a soft sedimentary rock called shale. When shale is pressed and heated, it hardens and turns to slate.

*Schoolchildren in some parts of the world, like this girl in India, still do their lessons on slates.*

Like most rocks, slate forms underground. Some rocks reach the surface when volcanoes blow their tops. Other rocks are shoved up from underground by earthquakes. The inside of Earth can be a very active place, with change taking place all the time.

*California's San Andreas Fault is the result of movement deep inside Earth.*

*Mount Whitney, in California, was formed when part of Earth's crust was thrust sharply upward.*

Forces within Earth make rocks move. They can push rock up to form mountains. Rocks atop the highest mountains might once have been buried beneath Earth's surface. Millions of years from now, the mountains will be worn away. Their rock may be buried again.

The next time you pick up a rock or look at one, remember that it has a story. Millions of years ago, it might have been formed in a fiery volcano, or on the bottom of a sea that has disappeared, or deep inside Earth when other rocks pressed down upon it. Sometime in the future, it will probably become another kind of rock.

Rocks may seem permanent, or changeless. But everything in our world changes, even rocks.

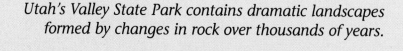

*Utah's Valley State Park contains dramatic landscapes formed by changes in rock over thousands of years.*

# Glossary

**fossils**—the remains of living organisms that have been preserved in rock

**igneous** (**ig**-nee-uhss) rock—a class of rock that forms from other rocks that have melted, then cooled and hardened

**metamorphic** (*met*-uh-**mor**-fik) rock—rocks that form from pressure and heat that was not enough to melt them

**minerals**—natural, nonliving substances with unique mixtures of chemicals

**pressure** (**presh**-ur)—the force that occurs when something is pushed down

**rock**—a solid mix of minerals

**sedimentary** (*sed*-uh-**men**-tuh-ree) rock—rock that has formed from particles that settle down, usually through water

# Index

basalt, 24

congomerate, 32

crust, 3–4

crystals, 10–14

    size, 12–13

elements, 10

eruption, 21

fossils, 34–37

gemstones, 14–16

    diamond, 16–18

    rubies, 15

gold, 14, 18

granite, 26–27

gypsum, 14

igneous rock, 20–27

    plutonic, 23, 26

    volcanic, 22–25

inner core, 6

jadeite, 14

lava, 21–22

limestone, 33

magma, 5, 21–22, 26

mantle, 5–6

marble, 40

metamorphic rock, 38–42

minerals, 8–9

    composition, 10

    crystal shape, 10

mountains, 43

olivine, 10

outer core, 6

pumice, 25

quartz, 10–11, 32

rhodonite, 14

rocks, formation of, 9

salt, 18

sediment, 28

sedimentary rocks, 20, 28–33

silver, 14

slate, 41

volcanoes, 42

# A Note to Parents

Learning to read is such an exciting time in a child's life. You may delight in sharing your favorite fairy tales and picture books with your child.

But don't forget the importance of introducing your child to the world of nonfiction. The ability to read and comprehend factual material will be essential to your child in school and throughout life. The Scholastic Science Readers™ series was created especially with beginning readers in mind. These books, with their clear texts and beautiful photographs, will help you to share the wonders of science with *your* new reader.

# Suggested Activity

Rock collecting is something everyone can enjoy! Many, many good books on this hobby are available for children, providing information on how to get started, how to figure out what sort of rocks might be found in your area of the country, and how to organize and store your collection.

Want a change from the rocks you are able to find on your own? Check out a Web site sponsored by the Smithsonian Institution's Department of Mineral Sciences. This site has photo galleries that highlight rocks, minerals, and gemstones found in the National Museum of Natural History:

**http://www.nmnh.si.edu/minsci**